Of Love With Love For Love

For Love

To Love, an endless journey.

Loyal

BookLeaf
Publishing

India | USA | UK

Made with ❤ on the BookLeaf Publishing Platform
www.bookleafpub.in
www.bookleafpub.com

Dedication

To love of all kinds!
To lovers of all times!
To nature and the universe,
Two of the biggest sources of love!
&
To my Beloved for life!

Preface

Love is the source of all goodness in this world. Every kindness we receive, no matter how small, carries its roots in some form of love — pure, hidden, or unspoken.

The poems you'll find here are written in both free verse and in more rigid forms, each carrying its own essence and rhythm. Some are brief, sharp as a spark, while others are longer, unfolding with patience yet holding strength within. The word Love in these pages is not bound to a single form or relationship — not merely romantic, nor familial, nor divine — but universal, vast enough to belong to every heart that reads these lines.

These poems span my journey as a writer, from my earliest attempts in 2017 to the more recent ones in 2025. They display, in their own quiet way, my evolution as a poet — sometimes hesitant, sometimes confident, but always sincere. Alongside them, you will also find a few poems written exclusively for this book, pieces that cannot be found anywhere else. I ask you to be kind to all of them, regardless of their polish, for each carries a fragment of who I was when I wrote it.

Most of the poems in this book are spontaneous outpourings, born in different seasons of my life, shaped by fleeting emotions, moments of silence, or sudden storms. Some of them even found their first breath in the fleeting space of Instagram stories, where they still linger in my highlight or posts — a kind of diary etched in pixels — before finding a lasting home here. Yet not all of these pieces carry such spontaneity; a few are deliberate, thought-through reflections.

At times, you may find a poem raw and realistic, carved with unshaken honesty. At other times, you may find a piece that exaggerates its ache or softens its truth. Both are true to me in their own way, for feelings are rarely precise.

I must offer an apology in advance: if any poem feels too close to your own wounds, if it unsettles or distresses, that was never my intent. Poetry often finds its reader in unexpected ways, and I hope mine meets you gently.

As my name suggests, I have tried to be Loyal at least to my poems — faithful to the emotions they carried, and honest n giving them the shape they deserved. My only hope is that I have done them justice.

Above all, I wish that the pain within these pages serves not to deepen sorrow, but to help heal it. May you leave these words carrying only love, in its purest and fullest form.

And lastly, thank you — for choosing to buy and hold a book of poems about love in these times. May it give you comfort, companionship, and perhaps even a little light. I'd be really happy to receive appreciation or feedback from you.

— Loyal (IG: @l_o.y.a_l)

Acknowledgements

To the woman I love the most — I am endlessly grateful to you for pouring into me enough love to write poems for many lifetimes. Your presence has been both muse and mirror. To my late brother — I thank you for the lessons your absence carved into me: pain, maturity, and responsibility. It was through that weight that I became a poet. To my late mother — of whom I carry bittersweet memories, yet whom I have loved unconditionally — thank you for the life and love that continue to echo within me. And to all the pets and puppies I've lost in the past, especially Mothi, Tommy, Gunda, Kukki, Pinky, Kempu, Softy and TPJ — I am grateful for the pawprints you've left on my heart, each one a reminder of innocence, loyalty, and unconditional love.

To my father, whom I continue to care for — I am grateful for your resilience, which teaches me strength each day. To my elder cousin, Alphu anna — thank you for your priceless support, a steadying hand through so many storms. To all my parents, whom I call Appa or Amma — especially Sara and

Lawrence — I am thankful for your blessings that flow silently through every page of this book.

To my friends — Sharlin, Madiha, Tasmiya, both Adithyas, Manoj, Nishanth, Chethan, Karan, Surya — and all other friends from past, present, and future: I am grateful for your companionship, which has been poetry in its own right. To all my sisters — Ina akka, Ivy akka, Rani akka, Nehu Didi, Anu akka, Nabha, Akshata, Kavya, Kavana, Kusuma, Saad Fathima, Salma Didi, Mahera Didi, Jayashree akka, and all my other sisters — thank you for your love, your guidance, and the ways you've stitched strength and tenderness into my life. To all my brothers, especially Vinu anna, Habeeb Anna, Subbanna, Adarsh Anna, my room mates Jackson Anna, Rahul Anna and Naveen Anna — I am grateful for your presence and the bonds that hold me steady. To my late grandparents — with special gratitude to my guiding spirit, Dr. Charles Dsouza — and to all my paternal uncles, aunts, cousins, nieces, and nephews, thank you for the roots and bonds that continue to shape me.

To all fellow poets of my generation, specially Swathi Pandit and Nabha Okkund — your poems have many a times sparked inspiration within me to write better. To my late uncle Jacob Lobo who handed me my early reads and inspired me initially into literature. And to his daughter Jaqueline Bai too for being an inspiration.

To my colleagues at Energage — especially my manager Syed Sir and system architect Kathir Sir, my team lead Parmeshwar Sir, and my entire team — I am grateful for your trust, patience, and encouragement along this journey. To those who raise their voices for the voiceless, and to all who love animals — I thank Nelson Sir from Shimoga for being such an inspiration, Ina akka for working so wonderfully to feed and care, Lekhana Jain whose love for animals I admire deeply, To Zoha Jung and The Backwater Sanctuary, one of a kind Equine rescue and rehabilitation centre for its kindness and to all animals at their jungle and city for filling my days with joy from far away, and Aashik Anna and his BeKind Foundation for their tireless compassion. To the Cutting Chai, Sahana Ram's Jimmy and all the lovely animals on the internet — I am grateful for the small joys you bring, brightening even the heaviest days. To my pets — Bhaira, Tinku, Gunda, and Kariya — and every animal on the street whom I've fed or patted: thank you for reminding me that love wears many forms, and often four paws.

To Dr. Ganesh Nayak, Dr. Pooja K and Sr. Zareena and other Nurses and all others at the hospital - Kiran Health Care, Thirthahalli — for the treatment and care I received for the infection I was going through, as I was finishing up my book. Your care and healing hands, kept me going and allowed me to complete this challenge on time.

To all those who've supported me as a poet across social media platforms — your encouragement has been a quiet light that kept me writing. To my family, and to anyone I may have missed — other than those I've missed with will — I am thankful for the ways, great and small, that you've been part of this journey. And finally, to all my literature teachers, to every poet and author I've read, to everyone who has supported me as a poet, and even to strangers I have met — thank you, for each of you has, in some way, contributed to these poems.

A small but heartfelt note of thanks also to Meta AI and ChatGPT, whose assistance in polishing and refining some of my poems gave me clarity in moments when words felt tangled. Their role has been like that of quiet companions — offering tools, never replacing my voice.

Special thanks to my favorite artist Sharlin Lawrence (IG: @scribblearts20_24) for designing a beautiful cover for this book, as a huge fan of your art and creativity. This is truly an honor for me. With deepest gratitude, to BookLeaf Publishing for this unique challenge and for giving me the opportunity to turn my words into this — my first book. Special thanks also to my Publishing Manager — Sapna Kumari from BookLeaf team, for helping me throughout the publishing process. To myself, for keeping up with this book and completing it through each thing that made it feel impossible.

And lastly, to all my readers — whether you are holding this book in your hands today, or whether you've read my poems time and time again across the internet — thank you. Each time you paused to read, reflect, or return to my words, you gave them a second life. Without you, these poems would remain whispers in my heart. With you, they breathe, they travel, and they belong to the world.

— Loyal

1. For My Love

You who call others ugly—
It is your mind that is stained.
If beauty is the measure of all,
What worth then is the heart's true feeling?
When the heart stops, beauty dies.

Charm is not what we inherit.
Even if gained, it fades—unnatural.
You who waste your hours on appearances, remember:
Wisdom is safer than skin,
And the love nurtured in the heart endures.

You judge by faces.
Yet in the womb, no one bore a shape.
If your mother had ended you
For being a formless child—
Would you have seen this tainted world,
Or admired your reflection at all?

Why bow to dust beneath the feet,
And never look within?
Think once with the heart:
Is a fair face enough,
If the soul inside is rotting?

Is skin color so mighty?
Is the cut of the face so grand?
Neither matters.
What matters is the mind at peace,
And thoughts in harmony with wisdom.

Beauty is easy to praise—
But greater still
Is to paint the portrait of a noble heart.
A lovely face may inspire a poem,
But a good heart writes endless prose.

You mocked the color of skin,
You laughed at the shape of bodies.
Why are your hearts so filthy?
You crushed innocent souls
Till they longed to end themselves.

The beauty of a face
Can be scarred with acid in a moment.
But nothing can scar
The beauty of a pure heart,
Or dim the light of a glorious mind.

2. Of Distant Love

The stars are far—
yet they light our nights.

The sun too keeps his distance,
yet he brightens our days.

The mountains lie beyond our reach,
yet their silent majesty gives us peace.

The horizon is but an illusion,
yet it beckons us to chase and explore.

And in life—
there are people who remain distant,
and others who live only in our minds—
imagined, remembered, or dreamed.
Yet they shape our days with beauty,
and sometimes with pain.

3. Wish With Love

Green, lush green farm,
And then the blue sky,
White and fluffy clouds—
Yes, fluffy clouds!
Not too scattered, not too dense!

The horizon is neither close,
nor is it distant.

The beach, the shore, and
the ocean lore;
And then the dark-blue sky,
The full moon and the clear sky,
full of stars—
You saw some of them fall!
You stood stunned; I made a wish.

I only made a wish for my dear,
forever wish with love!

4. Thought Of My Love

The serene sunset at the
sea shore,
The sky's layered with
pure gold,
The blissful sunrise on
a mountain peak,
The transition from dark
to light!

The flaming blaze of
fire,
The bright molten glass
cooling down,
The stardust spread
across the space,
The supernova and the
Saturn's rings,

The farthest galaxy and
the deepest ocean one
has ever seen!

And then there's the
thought of her on my mind!
It's beyond anything —
I could ever write!

5. Of Stars' Love

The stars,
They shine above—
Not for us,
But for themselves.

And yet we gaze,
And in that gaze,
We find love,
We find stories,
We find meaning.

We place upon them
Our hopes,
Our dreams,
Our pain.

They burn,
Unaffected,
But somehow—
They heal us.

6. Of All Love

Love is not about being captive,
Like the flower that offers itself to the bees—
Love is Dedication!

Love is not about being selfish,
Like the spider that becomes food for its young—
Love is Sacrifice!

Love is not about being angry,
Like the shore that embraces the waves which wear it
away—
Love is Patience!

Love is not about doubting,
Like the frog that sought shelter in the coils of a snake*—
Love is Belief!

Love is not about drifting apart,
Like the ants who toil together and share their meal—
Love is Compassion!

Love is not about punishing,
Like Christ forgiving those who crucified him—
Love is Forgiveness!

Love is not about ending,
Like pollen carried by the wind to distant lands—
Love is Infinity!

Love is not unnatural,
For it is Nature that first taught us to love—
Love is a Gift of Nature!

(* - Inspired by the story of Kappe Shankaralinga at
Sringeri, where even natural enemies reveal trust
through divine grace. The Kappe Shankara Temple is a
sacred site in Sringeri, Karnataka, dedicated to Lord
Shiva, known for a legend where Adi Shankara
witnessed a serpent shielding a pregnant frog from the
sun on the banks of the Tunga river.)

7. Measure Of Love

I started counting the stars—and lost count,
I started counting the grains of sand—and lost count,
I started counting the raindrops—and lost count,
I started counting the times I fell in love with you—
and I lost count!

I tried measuring the width of the universe—and failed,
I tried measuring the volume of the ocean—and failed,
I tried measuring the height of my dreams—and failed,
I tried to measure the depth of our love—
and I failed!

8. Madly With Love

Sitting on the brink of death,
While you stare into yourself,
You try not to fall,
While you fail to hold yourself from breaking down!

Days keep rolling,
Inside your brain's calendar,
While your heart's beating,
Beating out words like a painful drum!

Legs feel numb,
Hands don't stop
—Shaking—
From the loss of
—Everything—
You held so dear,
But now you fear!

In that pitch-black night,
You hope for a star,
You hope for Sun,
You seek for Moon,
You receive polaris at last!

11

The darkness still covers—
Your sight and it's still night,
But you now have a light!
But is it for this night?
Or will it finally last?
Last for years of light?

Slow count of stars,
You calm down at her feet,
The earth putting herself down,
To give you a place to stand on,
To live again!
A chance at life again!
Again! But one last time?!

———————————————————

Bonus:

When Death Smiled

I saw a smile on the death's face today!

- Loyal

9. For Love Alone

The nights are dark and there is daylight
It's one of the other and the other from the one
I've seen brighter nights and my days have lack light
For what I know there are more stars at night, day just
has one

I can fly high and reach the stars at night
I can dive deep in the morning to escape the light
I'm not afraid of heights nor does the depth scares me
yet
But I fear the heights that men can reach, how low one
can get

Nights of hunger, forest's silence and cities' crowd
Days that are scarier when hunter free to roam like prey
The lions roar, the sheeps mehh, and the humans pray
I don't trust the prey that prays for money, rather trust a
lion hunting for food

Yet in all this, Love lingers — unbroken, unseen,
A fire at night, a shade in the sun's keen.
It softens despair, it steadies my breath,
It gives both the hunter and hunted their depth.

Oceans roar louder at night, silenced at day?
Despair is roaming the beach, can it roar?
Breeze of night is not so cold for the day?
What are the day's typhoon at night calmed for?

There's **Dark & Light, Day & Night**, Hope & Despair —
where do I stand?
Leaning towards one or getting away, Love takes me by
the hand.
Evenings' Silverline shines for me,
For Love alone makes both night and day agree.

10. With Lost Love

Confession!

If I shall die anytime soon,
There wouldn't be any life in my body.
It might be very cold without the warmth —
Where could warmth be found at all?
Neither my soulmate's with me, nor my soul!

If I could still see the sky,
Would I tell the mourners a sweet lie?
Wouldn't I rather love to shout,
Try and tell the world how much I still love her!
If I could still talk before I fade in,
I'd wanna apologize to the flowers on my coffin.

Sorry, flowers — I don't have a soul!
I left it with her when I surrendered it.
If you were fortunate to hold her hand, or touch her sole,
You shall have some essence of it.

If I could still feel it again,
I would still feel the pain!

If I could still feel some pain,
I would take away the pain from the wood of my coffin.

11. Of ...lower's Love

Is there a choice for a flower —
To keep only butterflies of the daylight?
In the dark night, when an insect arrives,
Would it try to wush it away?

But I know for a reason:
A flower doesn't have a choice
But to bloom with nectar.

And if it's empty, or while it is refilling,
Would a hungry butterfly wait for the flower,
Merely out of love?

I respect its hunger
Much greater than love!
But my love —
Isn't the wait for your favorite nectar worth it?

No, it cannot always be so.
Sometimes, when it's about life and death,
Food, Freedom, Fun, and Fancy —
All come before love!

But wait...
Wh.... ab...... the ..lower?

12. All For Love

This street I'm walking through today,
The same street I've been walking since two falls,
Looks entirely different today!

It's all colorful — the lights of the night —
All bright and shiny, so welcoming,
But I'm so lost, I've become monochrome!

Without you, my life's, of course, colorless!
I keep my head down while I walk,
On the same street through which we used to talk.

The only two colors that are left —
The white kindness that's deeply rooted as I grew up,
The dark pain of everything that I can't give up.

I ate the food, but it didn't fill my stomach;
I fed a three-legged street dog —
His wiggling tail filled my empty soul a little.

I continued walking, looking back at him sitting
peacefully —
Again, the same colorless life,
Yet another end of day.

With every breath and every step, I want to end my life,
But I can't, for I know the pain I'd leave behind —
For you and the others who care —
The same pain I had to hide.

If the little hope keeps me alive,
I'll be grateful to you as long as I live;
Or I shall wait for a day when I have no one to leave.

13. With Love's Light

She came to my city
like a very bright star,
so bright,
I turned off all the little lights I had.

I've thrown them
into places I can't find them.
And now, if she wants to move out,
all that'll be left is darkness.

I didn't realise she was falling,
while the roof of suffering covered.
Could we ever know — at a glance —
if a star's just shooting,
or would it light up our sky for good?

Will the world be cruel
to expect from me —
to accept yet another star?
Let the world call me a fool
for keeping hope of my only star's comeback.

14. For Ever Love

The memories are the culprits,
Each time I feel like it's gone,
There comes another one,
Of you, my beloved.
With each passing wind and dust,
The moisture in the air,
The sky — both nights' and days' —
They remind me of you!
With each blink of each eye,
Each beat of the heart,
Each tap of my anxious feet,
Each pulse that runs through my veins,
Even when I fall short of breath —
My soul creates a fresh memory of you.
Doesn't matter if it's bitter or sweet,
It's still you, and only you!
For my soul keeps longing for
You — then, now, and forever!
I try to set them free,
But I've lost the key —
Never to be found ever!

15. Of Paws' Love & Of Love's Peace

I. Of Paws' Love

You adopted them!
And then,
There were these paws
You held,
And then,
They changed everything
About you.

And then,
You started living life,
Full spirit.
And then,
Each step of togetherness—
Pure magic.

And then,
As the bonding grew,
Your heart filled
With love—
Unconditional.

And then,
Those paws gave you peace,
Everlasting.
And then,
In the presence of that
Whirling tail,
All that pain from before—
Gone for good.

II. Of Love's Peace

Please, my soul,
Stay for a while.
Sit at that backwater.
Stop the self-quest.
Feel yourself.
Stop searching.

Find where you stand—
Right now is fine.
You are not who you were,
When we began this quest.

Do you still remember
What we were searching for?

But you are still here,
To me—
More near.

16. Of Beloved

Oh Beloved, I wandered,
All the streets of my city.
I knocked on each door,
Even the ones that lack a house!
I could still sense
Your presence in each one.
But since the time you left my city,
There isn't anyone left to open the doors.
And me — oh, I locked myself, and threw the key,
That day when my soul felt your love,
Into an abyss where my soul can never reach.
What more lesson is left to teach?

———

There was a storm,
A tsunami,
An earthquake,
A wildfire,
A volcanic eruption,
A blackout,
A drought,
And a flood,
In the city of my soul!

It still stands strong and still,
For it is built with kindness —
Of self and others,
And love of and for my beloved!

———

Oh Beloved, you plead with me,
To bury you in the graveyard of my city.
Yes, I have buried many people there —
But no matter what you or I do,
In my soul's city,
You remain — the only immortal being.

———

I'll write these poems,
Till I write a song someday —
One that resonates
All emotions into people.
And then I'll keep writing,
Till He finally stops
Breathing breath into this broken flute.

17. With/out Beloved

Oh Beloved, catch these tears of mine,
Not for they would turn into pearls,
Nor for it would lighten
the pain of my soul.
Catch them with your hands,
Let them stay worthy—
To wipe your own,
on that day when I'm finally gone
For my soul would die again and again,
lacking the hands
to wipe them.

———

And nothing was the same ever again—
Tears, hotter than Mercury.
Days, endless like Venus'.
Steps, heavier than Jupiter's weight.
Thoughts, spinning faster
than Saturn's last ring.
A heart, colder
than Uranus' dark night.
Hopes, drifting farther
than Neptune's edge.

Dreams, orphaned
like Pluto's exile.

And yet—
I bloom with life like Earth,
at times when we speak just sane.
I burn red like Mars,
each time I hear your name.

———

I want to fly,
till I see the depths no more.
I want to dive,
till I see the light no more.
I want to cry,
till I feel the pain no more.
I want to try,
till I fear to fail no more.
I want to be kind,
till I see the inhumane no more.
I want to love,
till I know the hate no more.

18. For Beloved

Dandelions and Daffodils,
Deadly fireflies start to kill.
If my dreams were true to be,
I'd be dead — or you'd still be here!

———

Oh Beloved, come, eat my soul
Before you drift away!
Don't leave behind even a small piece,
For the love that remains in it — it'll grow back,
Grow back to quest for you!
You'd find it filled with you again!

———

Oh Beloved, you ask me to take it easy —
Your departure from my life!
To me, whose soul drops and drops,
To undiscovered depths even,
When a dog which wagged its tail,
Later turns its back
When I whistle at it!

———

Oh Beloved, take my hand and pull me out,
From this deep darkness you left me in.
Pull me before you find peace without me up there,
Or pull me before I find pseudo peace
In this abyss here!

19. Of Love!

There could be nothing more,
There could be an evermore too.
There are things that worry you —
Are there things that make you happy?

I ask,
can I be a part of your life?
To worry you, or to make you happy —
but more,
to be by your side when you're happy
and when you're worried.

I become an annoyance,
make you more worried when you already are,
steal the joy from your moments — I'm greedy.
Yet, all I really want
is to calm you when you're worried,
to show you more love in your happiest times —
to make you happier.

But I fail, fail, and fail.
Still, I try, try, and try.
All I want for myself — is to not let you down.
All I want for you — is to not let go of yourself.

And then there's love —
that we've treasured since a long time.
The relationship may become messy,
confused, spoiled, spilt,
rotten, or even dead —

But love —
is eternal,
and my soul.

I could never, ever give up on love,
and love alone.
Not me,
not you —
but only love,
that brought us together.

Love!

20. With Love!

I wonder how I lose words when I see you.
I can write poems and stories, and what not —
Why am I not able to convey my feelings?
Why do I always mess up with the words I choose?
Why can't I confess my love for you — in words?

Here, I use this poem With Love —
A selfish poet, I am —
To confess my love,
To confess my feelings,
To confess my apologies,
To confess how much I care.

My love for you is endless,
My feelings for you are true.
My apologies are selfless —
I'll forever and ever care for you,
With Love!

21. For Love!

One random day — two souls meet,
Both vulnerable, yet strong.
One of you — strong enough to open up vulnerable,
And you — whose vulnerability is a strength.

And in days, your souls
Crave for each other,
Seeking to listen,
Seeking to tell —
Your stories to one another.

You find solace
In togetherness —
The joy of having a soul
That could feel your pain.
You accept them as they are,
They accept you as you seemed.

The guilty is the one —
Who only understood,
But didn't care to be understood.
You wanted to be a safe place,
To give them comfort —
While forgetting your own.

It's true that the pain
Of your beloved felt more —
More than your own.
And you hid things from them,
Things that could hurt them more —
Of past and of present,
Of situations
That made you a sinner.

And you — loved the warmth,
Loved everything your beloved gave you:
From time to things,
From a shoulder to cry on
To a mind that listened,
From support to care,
The provision of the provider.
From lessons to life —
Both making and breaking.

Your soul drifted into a comfortable sleep.
You gave things in return,
Some without asking,
Some after begging.
Things like —
Support, care, and understanding.
And people like —

Mother, father, sisters, and friends.
A world enough to live indeed.

Both were cursed by the blessing
Of not being able to live by self.
Both gifted abundantly —
Memories enough for a lifetime,
Griefs enough till graves.

You made promises,
You broke promises.
You made memories,
You cherish memories.
You made wishes,
You lived wishes.
You made plans,
You lived plans.
You saw dreams,
You lived dreams.
You had fights,
You resolved fights.
You forgave leaving behind the pain,
You forgave holding onto the pain.
There were many painful departures,
And so were many joyful arrivals.
You witnessed together the happiness of births,
And shared the sorrows of deaths.

You stood together —
Through all the difficult times.
You still do — but...

Both in a different loop.

Your love grew stronger —
More than it should have.
So strong it choked
The one whom you'd never wish to hurt.
Strong like a Carbon–Carbon bond —
Unable to accept space;
Let alone distance — was pain.

And you — your pain grew larger,
Larger than life itself.
You held onto love
To bear the pain.
And when love gave more pain,
You let go — dead from within —
To hold onto life again.
You're healing for a lifetime,
Still afraid of the past pain —
A pain you'll never be able to let go.
You left behind pain —
Unhealable with time.

You hold onto the same love,
Unable to let go of love —
Love that's hurting you.
Love from which
You don't want to heal.
But —
Of love, you write.
With love, you care.
For love, you stay here —
In an empty world, that is rare.

You both are drained, yet filled with love.
You live with hopes
That healing will come.
The pain of past is at the shore,
You see tears but can't console.
Both choose paths —
Different kinds,
Both true like paradise.
You loved so much you can't unlove,
No matter the hurt.
You loved so much you fear love,
So much was hurt.

All this you still do —
Known and unknown —
For love that is overdue,

For love that is true,
For love that is you,
For Love!...

www.ingramcontent.com/pod-product-compliance
Lightning Source LLC
Chambersburg PA
CBHW070459050426
42449CB00012B/3051